5/2/13

Louisburg Library
Library District No. 1, Miami County
206 S. Broadway, Louisburg, KS 66053
913-837-2217
www.louisburglibrary.org

Clownfish

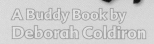

A Buddy Book by
Deborah Coldiron

ABDO
Publishing Company

UNDERWATER WORLD

Louisburg Library
Bringing People and Information Together

VISIT US AT
www.abdopublishing.com

Published by ABDO Publishing Company, 8000 West 78th Street, Edina, Minnesota 55439.

Printed in the United States.

Coordinating Series Editor: Sarah Tieck
Contributing Editor: Michael P. Goecke
Graphic Design: Deborah Coldiron
Cover Photograph: Photos.com
Interior Photographs/Illustrations: Brandon Cole Marine Photography (pages 13, 19, 22, 23); Clipart.com (page 11); GeoAtlas (page 9); Minden Pictures: Fred Bavendam (page 28), Norbert Wu (page 17); Photos.com (pages 5, 15, 24, 30); SeaPics.com: Espen Rekdal (page 29); Wikipedia.org - Wikipedia Commons: Haplochromis (pages 7, 21), Hans Hillewaert (page 25), Uwe Kils (page 25), National CSIRO Center (page 27)

Library of Congress Cataloging-in-Publication Data

Coldiron, Deborah.
  Clownfish / Deborah Coldiron.
    p. cm. -- (Underwater world)
  Includes index.
  ISBN 978-1-60453-130-5
  1. Anemonefishes--Juvenile literature. I. Title.

  QL638.P77C65 2008
  597'.72--dc22

                                                              2008005044

Table Of Contents

The World Of Clownfish

Every living creature needs water. Some animals not only need water, they live in it, too.

Scientists have found more than 250,000 kinds of plants and animals living underwater. And, they believe there could be one million more! The clownfish is one animal that makes its home in this underwater world.

Water covers 70 percent of Earth's surface.

Clownfish are small, saltwater fish. They live among sea anemone **tentacles**. Clownfish are known for their bright orange bodies. They also have thick white stripes outlined in black.

Sea anemone tentacles can sting powerfully. But, they do not harm clownfish.

Clownfish are found in the **tropical** areas of the Indian and Pacific oceans. They live in Australia's Great Barrier **Reef**, too. Clownfish are also found in the Red Sea, between Africa and Asia.

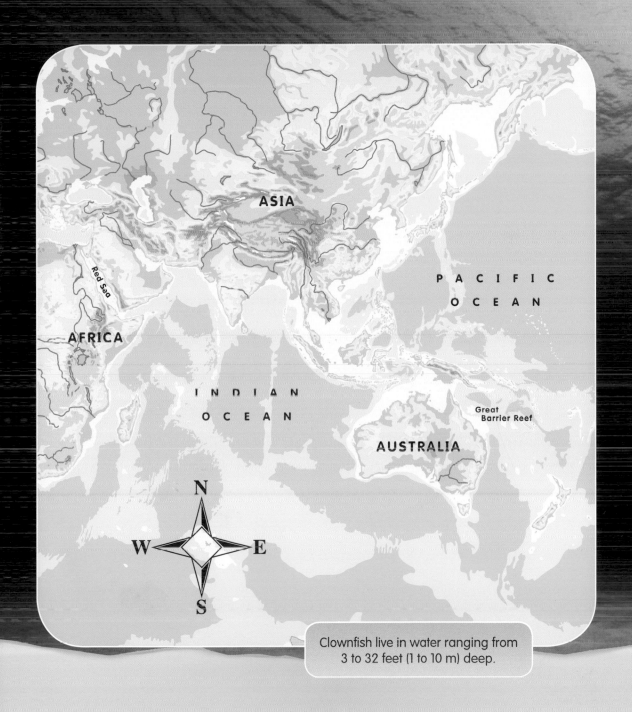

ASIA

Red Sea

PACIFIC
OCEAN

AFRICA

INDIAN
OCEAN

Great
Barrier Reef

AUSTRALIA

N

W   E

S

Clownfish live in water ranging from
3 to 32 feet (1 to 10 m) deep.

A Closer Look

A clownfish has two fins on its belly and one long fin on its back. The clownfish also has a fin on each side. The fins work together to allow the clownfish to move quickly and easily.

FAST FACTS Clownfish are vertebrates. This means they have a backbone.

The Body Of A Clownfish

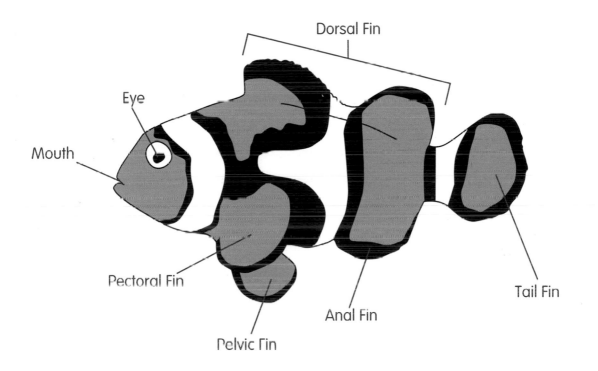

Clownfish are very active. These small, forceful fish dart in and out of anemone **tentacles**. And, they challenge larger fish that nibble on their **hosts**.

Divers often confuse clownfish movement for play. But, they are actually protecting and caring for their homes.

A Special Relationship

Clownfish benefit from living with sea anemones. And, sea anemones benefit from clownfish.

For example, a clownfish tidies up after an anemone's dinner. And, it eats dead anemone **tentacles**. This means the anemone stays healthy, while the clownfish gets a meal.

FAST FACTS There are more than 1,000 different species of sea anemones. But, only ten species can host clownfish.

14

Sea anemones look like underwater plants. But, they are actually animals. They are closely related to jellyfish and coral.

A clownfish benefits from the safe shelter of a sea anemone's stinging **tentacles**. And, the sea anemone benefits from the clownfish's bravery. A clownfish protects its **host** when predators come too close.

Some clownfish call the magnificent anemone home. These giant anemones can grow to be three feet (1 m) wide!

A Growing Clownfish

A female clownfish may **spawn** at any time of the year. The process begins when a male clears a space for a nest. Clownfish often make nests on flat pieces of rock or coral near their **hosts**.

Clownfish grow to be two to three inches (5 to 8 cm) in length. Female clownfish are usually larger than males.

Next, the female lays her eggs on the nest. She may lay up to 1,000 eggs at a time. The male protects her while she works. Then, he **fertilizes** the eggs and guards them until they hatch.

After hatching, the tiny clownfish larvae (LAHR-vee) float toward the surface. They drift there for a few weeks. Then, the strong, young clownfish return to the ocean floor. There, they find anemone **hosts**.

A male clownfish carefully looks after the fertilized eggs. He constantly cleans the eggs until they hatch.

Family Connections

Clownfish are also known as clown anemonefish. They are one of 27 **species** of anemonefish.

Anemonefish come in a wide variety of bright colors and patterns. They all rely on sea anemones for shelter and protection.

Pink anemonefish grow to about four inches (10 cm) long.

Red saddleback anemonefish are dark orange. They have a black spot, or saddle, on either side of their bodies. Their young have a single white band instead of the black marks.

Spine-cheek anemonefish have a pair of small spines just below their eyes. Females change from bright orange to a reddish brown or black color as they age. So, they are also called maroon clownfish.

A false clown anemonefish looks a lot like a true clownfish. But, it has thinner or no black borders on its white stripes.

Orange-fin anemonefish have brown or black bodies. Their faces and fins are yellowish orange. And they have a white tail. Their young are a dull orange color.

Dinnertime

Clownfish eat the leftovers and dead **tentacles** of their anemone **hosts**. They also eat **algae**, **zooplankton**, and shellfish.

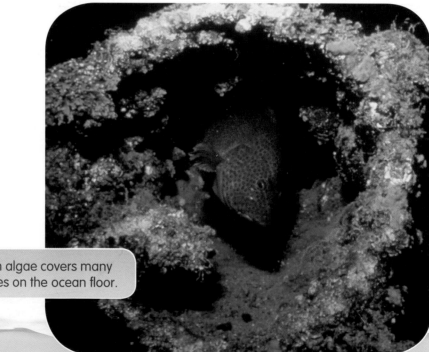

Green algae covers many surfaces on the ocean floor.

Zooplankton includes tiny copepods *(above)* and isopods *(below)*. These animals are important to a clownfish's diet.

A World Of Danger

Many ocean creatures avoid clownfish because of their stinging **hosts**. Still, others do eat them.

Humans are the clownfish's worst enemy. Many people keep them in home aquariums.

Some pet store suppliers raise clownfish. This helps protect wild populations from human predators.

Fascinating Facts

Clownfish live in groups. A large female is **dominant**. All clownfish are born male. As they age, they can become females. This will happen if the dominant female dies.

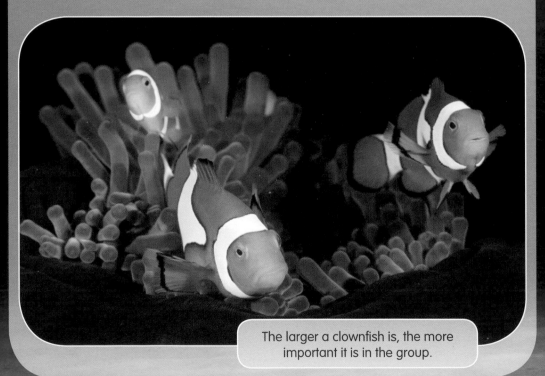

The larger a clownfish is, the more important it is in the group.

Clownfish larvae often drift far away from their birthplace. However, scientists recently discovered that more than half return to their birthplace as adults. There, the clownfish live and **spawn**.

Anemonefish larvae are very small. Many do not survive in the wild.

Learn And Explore

How do clownfish live among sea anemones without being stung? Some scientists discovered skin **mucus** provides protection. Others found answers in **algae** on clownfish scales.

By studying clownfish, scientists are learning how to protect humans from stinging organisms. Their research has already helped create two successful jellyfish **repellent** creams!

Jellyfish and sea anemones are closely related stinging organisms.

IMPORTANT WORDS

alga a plant or plantlike organism that lives mainly in the water.

dominant commanding, controlling, or ruling over all others.

fertilize to make fertile. Something that is fertile is capable of growing or developing.

host a living plant or animal on or in which an organism lives.

mucus thick, slippery fluid from the body.

reef an underwater ridge of rock, coral, or sand.

repellent something that repels, or resists.

spawn to produce eggs.

species living things that are very much alike.

tentacle a long, slender body part that grows around the mouth or the head of some animals.

tropical having warm temperatures.

zooplankton small animals that float in a body of water.

WEB SITES

To learn more about clownfish, visit ABDO Publishing Company on the World Wide Web. Web sites about clownfish are featured on our Book Links page. These links are routinely monitored and updated to provide the most current information available.

www.abdopublishing.com

INDEX